INDEX

DEEP RIVER

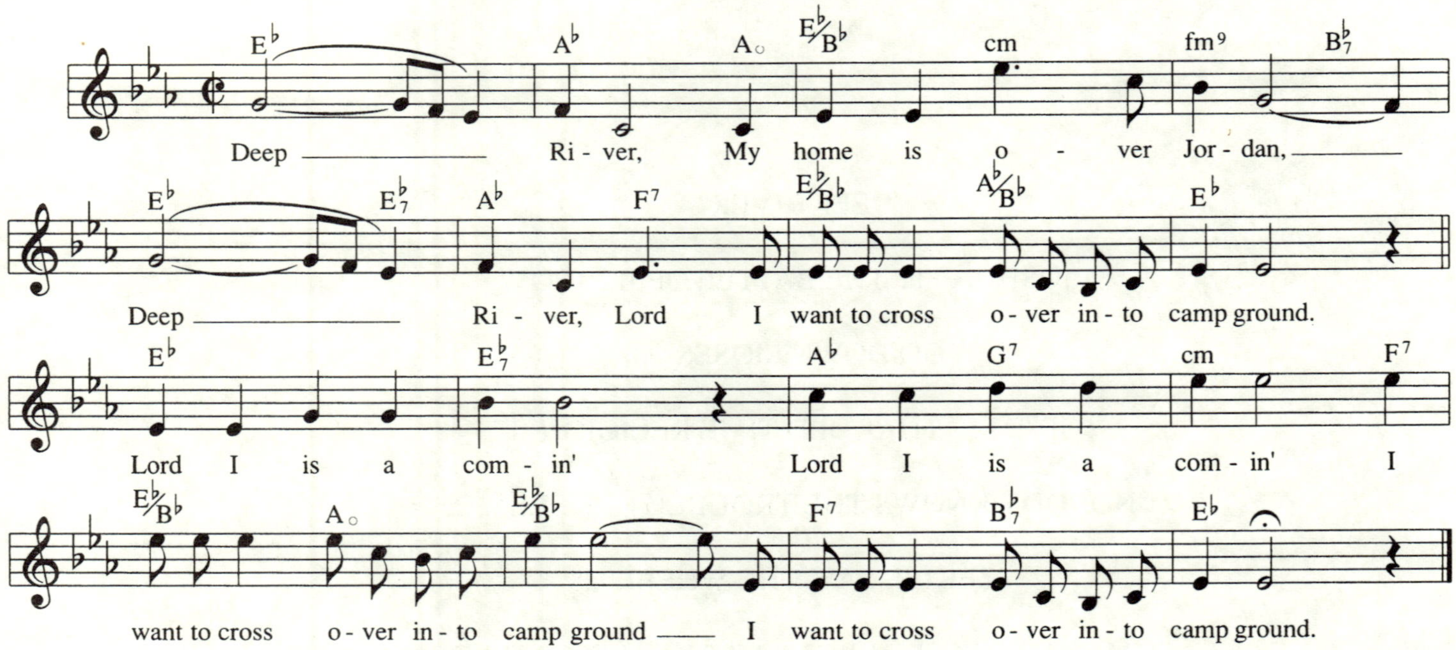
Deep River, My home is over Jordan,
Deep River, Lord I want to cross over into camp ground.
Lord I is a comin' Lord I is a comin' I
want to cross over into camp ground I want to cross over into camp ground.

Moderato
mp espr. cantabile
5
8
poco cresc.
poco rit.
mf
Tempo I

13
p
17
21
25
cresc.
29
f
sub. p
8vb

33
dolce
p
mp
37
cresc.
41
mf
p
poco
8va
45
cresc.
decresc.
8va
49
poco rit.
p

JOSHUA FIT THE BATTLE OF JERICO

dm A7 dm
Josh - ua fit the batt - le ob Je - ri - co, Je - ri - co, Je - ri - co,
dm dm/C dm/B B♭ dm/A A7 dm
Josh - ua fit the batt - le ob Je - ri - co, And the walls came tumb - ling down. You may
(Fine)
dm gm/E A7 dm
talk a - bout your king of Gi - de - on, You may talk a - bout your man of
to the walls of Je - ri - co, He marched with spear in
lamb - ram sheep - horns be - gin to blow, Trum - pets be - gin to
gm/E A7 dm dm/C dm/B B♭
Saul, There's none like good old Josh - ua at the
hand. Go, blow them ram - horns Josh - ua cried cause the
sound. Josh - ua comman - ded the chil - dren to shout and the
dm/A A7 1-2. dm 3. dm
batt - le of Je - ri - co. Up
batt - le is in my hand. Then the
walls came tum - bling down.

Allegretto
mf
5

9
cresc.
f
13
p
sfz
sfz
sfz
17
f
sub. p
f
21
p
25
cresc.
f
p
sfz

29
p
sfz
sfz
32
sfz
cresc.
35
cresc.
f
cresc. molto
38
sub. p
ff
42
cresc.
sforzando
sub. p
f

46
f
p
50
f
p
54
sub. f
sub. p
58
62
Rubato
8vb

GO DOWN MOSES

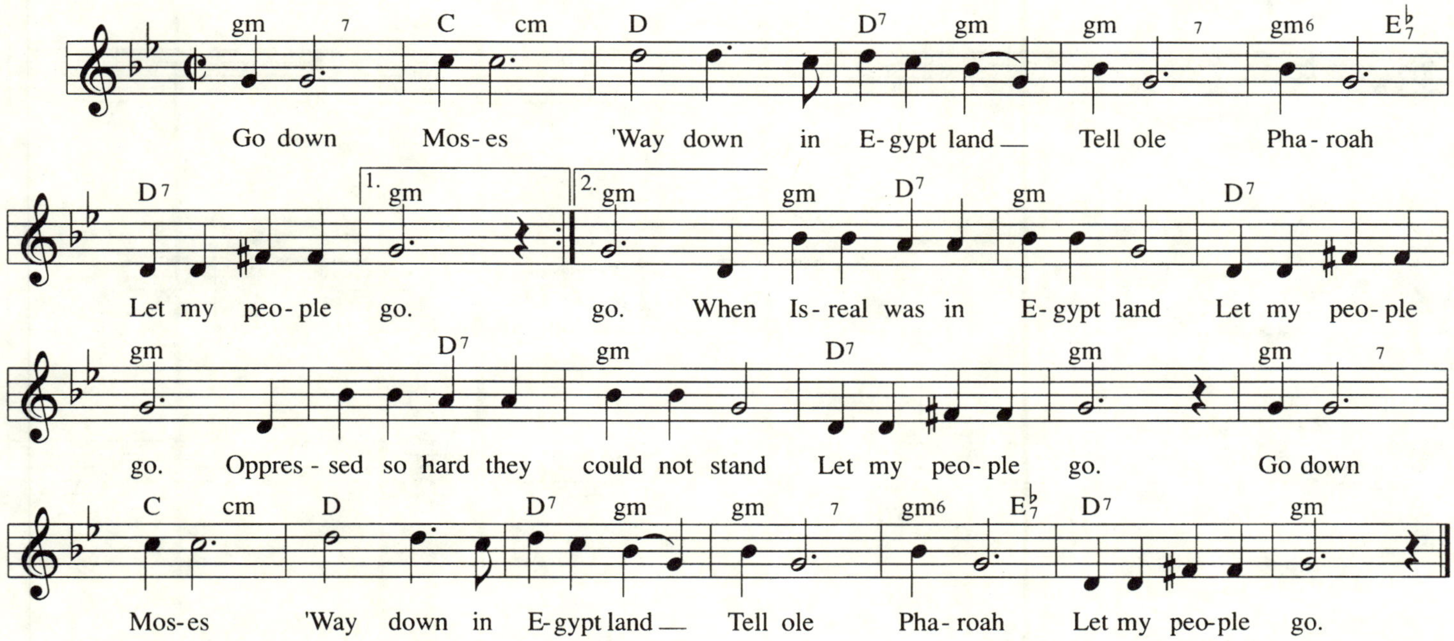
gm 7 C cm D D7 gm gm 7 gm6 E♭7
Go down Mos-es 'Way down in E-gypt land — Tell ole Pha-roah
D7 1. gm 2. gm gm D7 gm D7
Let my peo-ple go. go. When Is-real was in E-gypt land Let my peo-ple
gm D7 gm D7 gm gm 7
go. Oppres-sed so hard they could not stand Let my peo-ple go. Go down
C cm D D7 gm gm 7 gm6 E♭7 D7 gm
Mos-es 'Way down in E-gypt land — Tell ole Pha-roah Let my peo-ple go.

Rubato
mp
rit.
4
Andante
8

12
legato
espressivo
15
18
f
22
p
f
26
p
mp cantabile
8vb

30
cresc.
33
poco rit.
Tempo I
mf
decresc.
p
37
Quasi rubato
mp
40
43
poco cresc.

46
cresc.
decresc.
49
p
52
f
p
56
f
p
61

64
67
mf
70
73
cresc.
76
decresc.

79
82
f
85
p
f
89
93
mp
8vb
97
rit.
rubato

GIVE ME THAT OLD TIME RELIGION

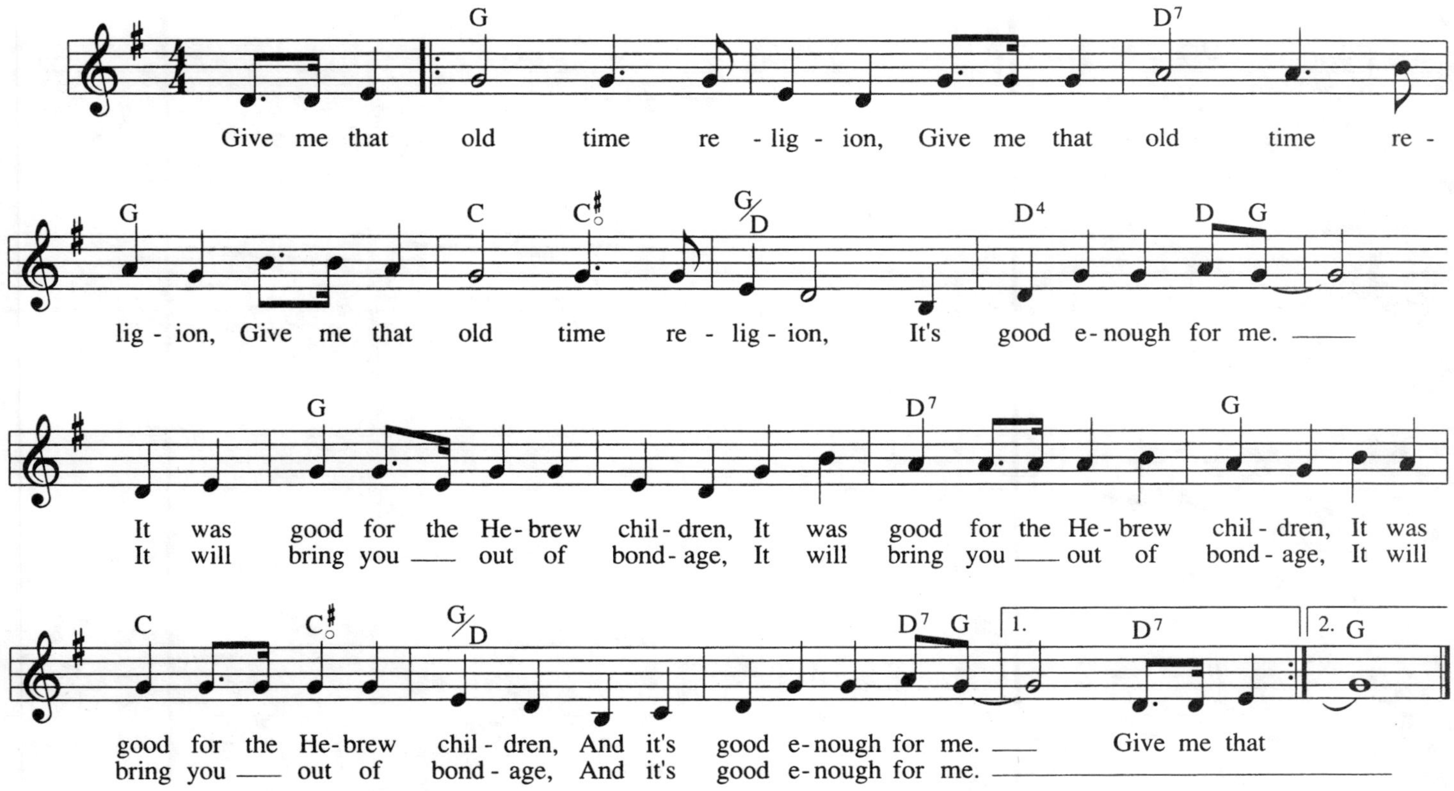
G D7
Give me that old time re - lig - ion, Give me that old time re -
G C C♯o G/D D4 D G
lig - ion, Give me that old time re - lig - ion, It's good e - nough for me.
G D7 G
It was good for the He - brew chil - dren, It was good for the He - brew chil - dren, It was
It will bring you out of bond - age, It will bring you out of bond - age, It will
C C♯o G/D D7 G 1. D7 2. G
good for the He - brew chil - dren, And it's good e - nough for me. Give me that
bring you out of bond - age, And it's good e - nough for me.

Allegro
p
5
cresc.
f

10
15
19
3
sub. p
23
f
(♯)
27
3

31
p
35
f
38
41
ff
mp
ff
sfz
45
mf
cresc.
f

48
p
53
cresc.
f
58
63
ff
sfz
mp
67
sfz
p
cresc.

71
f
sfz
mp
sfz
74
sfz
sfz
f
78
p cantabile
82
88

94
f
98
102
accelerando
107
molto accelerando
Lento
112
poco rit.
Tempo I
8vb

NOBODY KNOWS THE TROUBLE I'VE SEEN

D G D E7 A7
No - bod - y knows the trou ble I've seen, No - bod - y knows but Je - sus.
D G F♯ bm D/A A7 D
No - bod - y knows the trou ble I've seen, Glor - y Hal - le - lu - jah! Some - times I'm up, some -
f♯m bm7 E7 A D D7 GMaj 9 gm Maj 7 D/A A7 D
times I'm down Yes! Yes! Lord some - times I'm al - most to the ground Yes! Yes! Lord!

Andante, quasi rubato
mf
espressivo, legato
cresc.
decresc.

p

34
38
42
cresc.
46
decresc.
p
50
poco rit.
cresc.

54
decresc.
tr
cresc.
58
6
tenuti
f espr.
61
64
67

70
73
decresc.
mp
76
cresc.
19
79
f
rit.
Tempo I
mf
82
maestoso
p
mf

'ZEKIEL SAW THE WHEEL

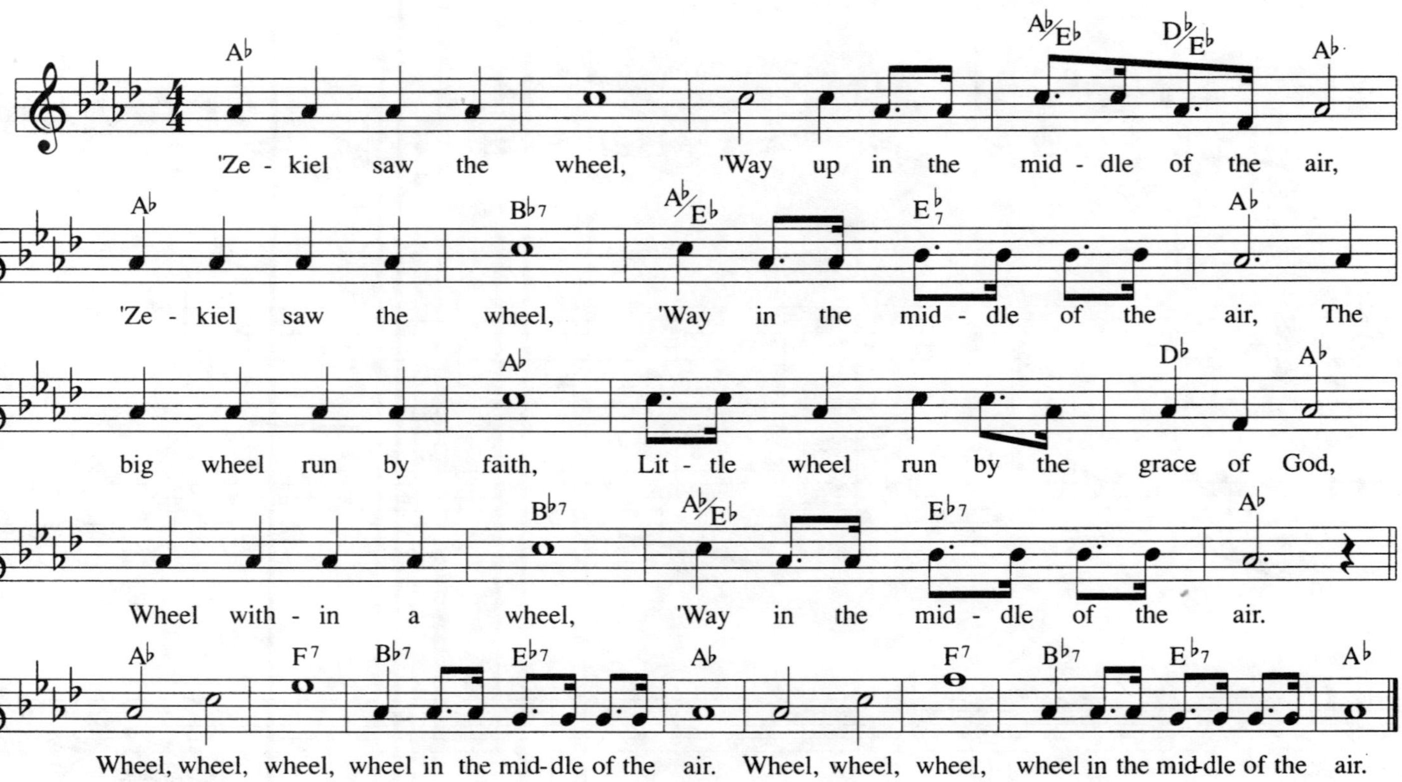
'Ze - kiel saw the wheel, 'Way up in the mid - dle of the air,
'Ze - kiel saw the wheel, 'Way in the mid - dle of the air, The
big wheel run by faith, Lit - tle wheel run by the grace of God,
Wheel with - in a wheel, 'Way in the mid - dle of the air.
Wheel, wheel, wheel, wheel in the mid- dle of the air. Wheel, wheel, wheel, wheel in the mid-dle of the air.

Moderato
tenuto
mf

13
cresc.
17
f
21
25
p grazioso
29

33
ff
37
poco cresc.
decresc.
41
tr
45
cresc.
mf
p
49
f
3
8vb

53
sub. p
57
61
cresc.
65
f
69
poco rit.
rubato

SOMETIMES I FEEL LIKE A MOTHERLESS CHILD

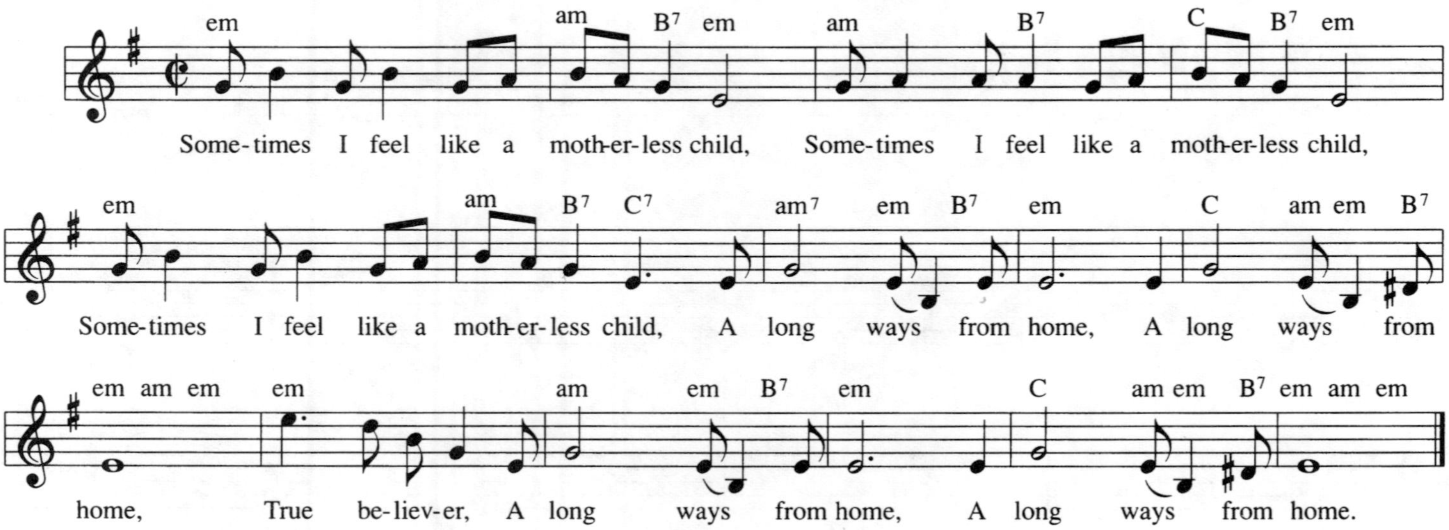
em am B7 em am B7 C B7 em
Some-times I feel like a moth-er-less child, Some-times I feel like a moth-er-less child,
em am B7 C7 am7 em B7 em C am em B7
Some-times I feel like a moth-er-less child, A long ways from home, A long ways from
em am em em am em B7 em C am em B7 em am em
home, True be-liev-er, A long ways from home, A long ways from home.

Andante, cantabile
p
poco cresc.
decresc.
cresc.

13
rit.
3
f
17
decresc.
21
cresc.
poco rit.
decresc.
25
p legato
8vb
29
poco cresc.
8vb

33
mf sempre cresc.
37
sempre cresc.
f
rit.
8vb
42
Tempo I
sub. p
rit.
decresc.
molto rit.
pp
47
Tempo I
mf agitato
cresc.
50
cresc.
poco rit.
f
53
rubato
mf
Tempo I
rit.
decresc.
8vb

DOWN BY THE RIVERSIDE

G C cm G
1. Gwine-a lay down mah bur - den Down by the ri-ver-side,
D7 G C cm
Down by the ri-ver-side, Down by the ri-ver-side, lay down mah bur-den,
G am7 D7 G Fine
Down by the ri-ver-side, To stu - dy war no mo'!
C G
put on mah long white robe, Gwine - a put on mah star-ry crown, Gwine - a
lay down mah sword an' shield, Gwine - a put on mah star-ry crown, Gwine - a
am D7 G 1. G7 2. D7
stu - dy war no mo'! I'm gwine - a 2. Gwine-a
stu - dy war no mo'!

Allegro
p
5

9
13
17
mp
sfz
21
sfz
25
sfz

29
cresc.
f
34
39
44
8vb
48
sfz
sub. p

52
56
61
65
mp
70

74
78
3
f
82
86
sub. p
90
cresc.
f

94
p
98
103
cresc.
mf
3
107
p
mf
112
f

116
120
sub. p
cresc.
124
f
128
f
132

136
140
8va
mp
cresc.
145
f
149
153

157
p
161
165
169
3
3
173
p
f
p

177
legato
181
184
sub. f
188
tenuti
8vb
8vb
8vb
193
cresc.

IT'S A ME, O LORD

C G7 C F G C
It's a me It's a me O Lord, stand-in' in the need of prayer. It's a
E7 am D7 G7 C F
me It's a me O Lord stand-in' in the need of prayer. Not my broth-er, it's a
C7 F C G7 C F E7 am D7
me O Lord. Not my sis-ter it's a me O Lord, stand-in' in the need of prayer,
C/G G7 C G7 C F G
stand-in' in the need of prayer. It's a me It's a me O Lord, stand-in' in the need of
C E7 am D7 G7 C
prayer. It's a me It's a me O Lord, stand-in' in the need of prayer.

Rubato
mf
4

poco rit.
Tempo I
p
poco cresc.
decresc.
Andante
mp legato

26
29
32
8va
mf
mp
35
p
cresc.
38
sub. p

poco rit.
cresc.
Tempo I
Agitato
Più mosso
mf

poco rit.
meno mosso
decresc.
Rubato
rit.
Lento

WERE YOU THERE

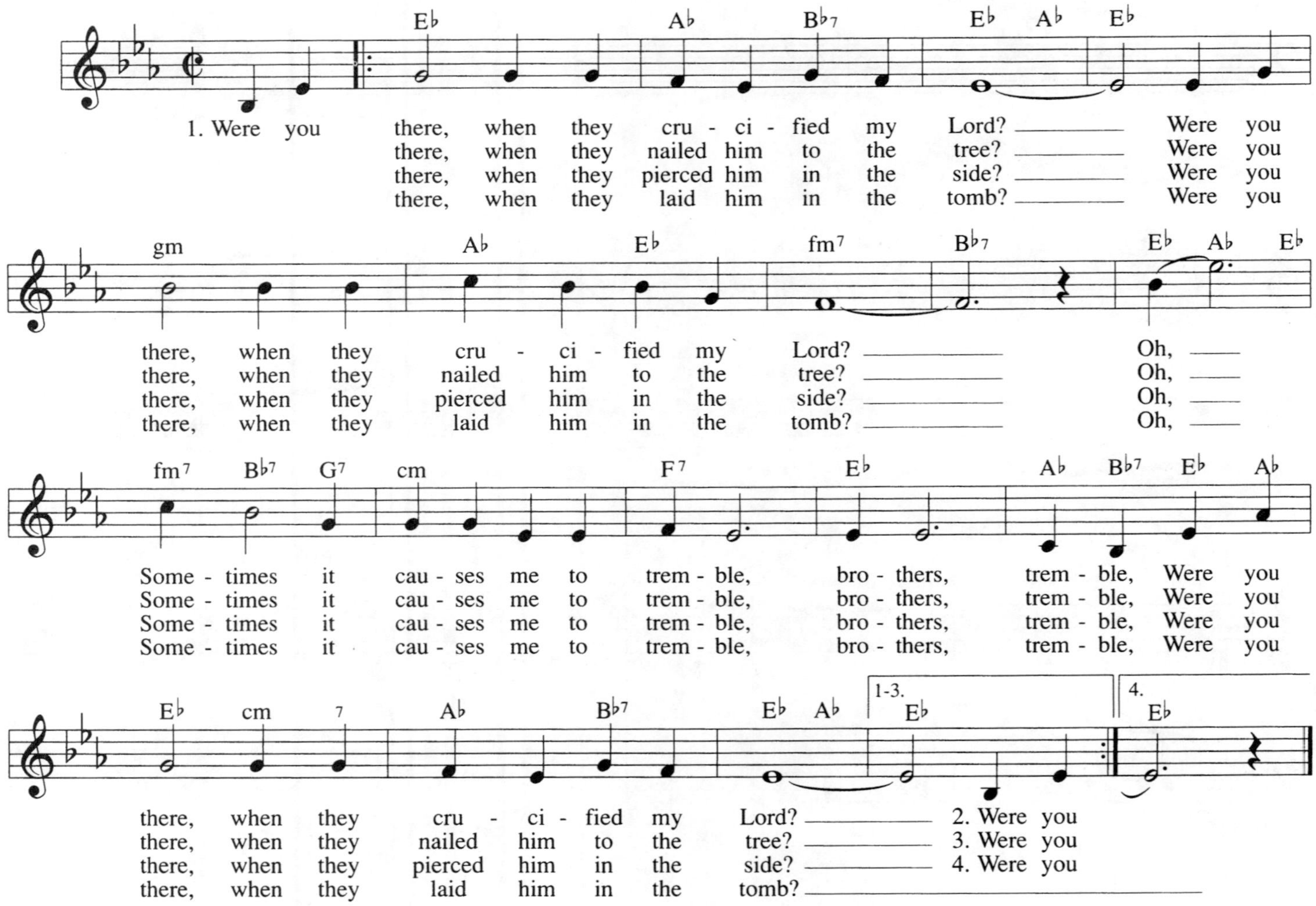

10
15
19
24
sfz
f
28

32
p dolce
37
42
46
cresc.
sub. p
50
f

55
59
sfz
63
68
rit.
73
Maestoso
tenuti
rit.

I WANT TO BE READY

D D7 G G♯ D/A D
I want to be read - y, I want to be read - y,
A F♯ bm D/A G/A D G D
I want to be read - y to walk in Je - ru - sa - lem, just like John. 1. John
2. When
D F♯7 bm D/A G/A D G
said the cit - y was just four - square, Walk in Je - ru - sa - lem just like John, And
Peter was preach - ing at Pen - te - cost, Walk in Je - ru - sa - lem just like John, He
D F♯7 bm E7 G D
he de - clared he'd meet me there, Walk in Je - ru - sa - lem, just like John.
was en - dowed with the Ho - ly Ghost, Walk in Je - ru - sa - lem, just like John.

Allegro
f
6
10

15
p
20
25
29
cresc.
sf
sub. p
33
sub. f
sfz
mp

38
molto legato, cantabile
43
47
poco rit.
51
rit.
cresc.
55
Maestoso

ROLL JORDAN ROLL

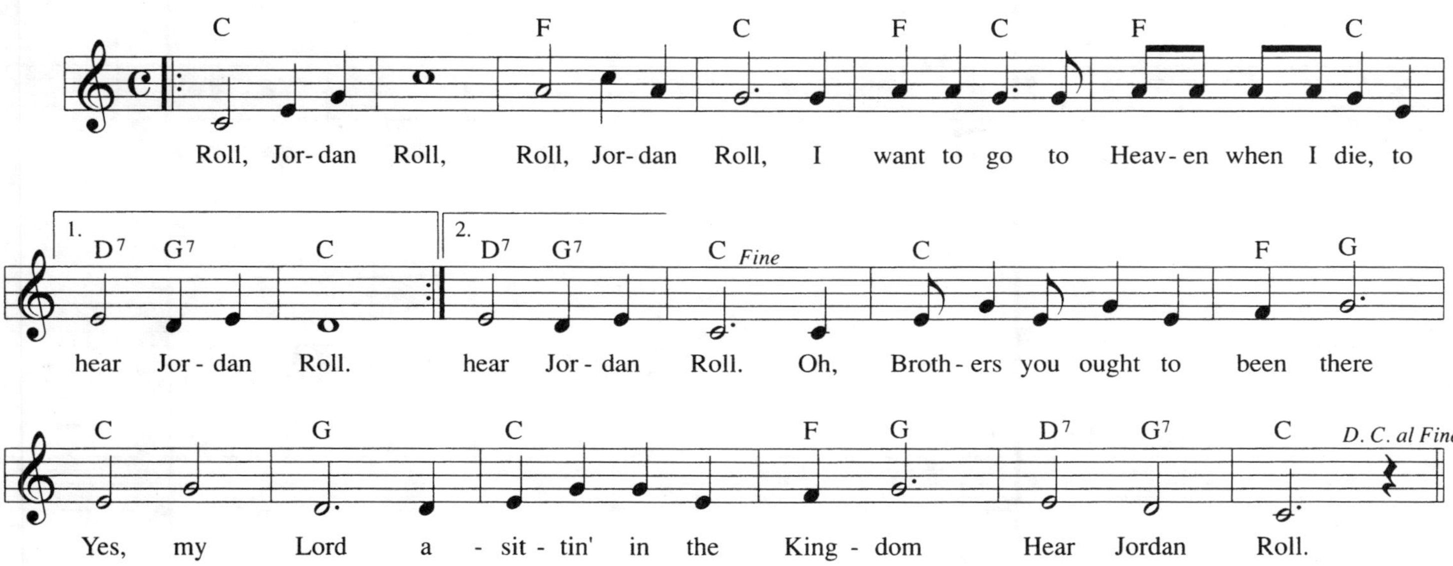
C F C F C F C
Roll, Jor- dan Roll, Roll, Jor- dan Roll, I want to go to Heav- en when I die, to
1. D7 G7 C
2. D7 G7 C Fine C F G
hear Jor- dan Roll. hear Jor- dan Roll. Oh, Broth- ers you ought to been there
C G C F G D7 G7 C D. C. al Fine
Yes, my Lord a - sit - tin' in the King - dom Hear Jordan Roll.

Rubato
p
5
9

13
17
21
25
p
29

33
Allegretto tenuti
mf
cresc.
36
cresc.
f
sub. p
40
poco rit.
Tempo I
p
44
poco cresc.
47
p

51
cresc.
54
57
p
60
poco rit.
64

MICHAEL ROWS THE BOAT

D G D
1. Mi-chael rows the boat a - shore, Hal - le - lu - ja! Mi - chael
blows the trum - pet - horn, Hal - le - lu - ja! Trum - pet
stream is deep and wide, Hal - le - lu - ja! Je - sus
A E7 A7 1-2. D 3. D
boats a Gos - pel boat. Hal - le - lu - ja. 2. Ga - briel
sounds the world a - round. Hal - le - lu - ja. 3. Jor - dan's
stands on the other side. Hal - le - lu - ja.

11
Andante
mf
15
19

23
27
mp
31
Leggiero
35
39

43
46
poco rit....
p cantabile
50
54
58

62
mf
66
71
76
rit.
Maestoso
cresc.
f
80
rit.

I'VE BEEN IN THE STORM SO LONG

cresc.
sub. p
mf
cresc.
f

25
mp
f
29
mp
33
sfz
37
cresc.
p
41
45
cresc.
cresc.
rit.
f
p
Lento

HE'S GOT THE WHOLE WORLD IN HIS HANDS

G G C G D7
He's got the whole world in His hands; He's got the whole wide world
G G C G D7
in His hands; He's got the whole world in His hands; He's got the whole world in His
G G G C G
hands. He's got the earth and sky in His hands; He's got the
D7 D7 G
night and day in His hands; He's got the sun and moon
G C G D7 G
in His hands; He's got the whole world in His hands. He's got the

Moderato
mf
4

8
11
14
17
20

f
p

38
41
tr
44
f
47
50
p

53
57
cresc.
f
61
65
p
69
f
ff
sfz
sfz

SWING LOW, SWEET CHARIOT

F gm7 C7 F gm7 C7
Swing low, sweet char - i - ot, Com-in' for to car - ry me home,
F F7 B♭ C dm G7 C7 F
Swing low, sweet char - i - ot Com- in' for to car - ry me home. I
F A♭o gm C7 F am gm7 C7
look'd o- ver Jor - dan and what did I see? Com- in' for to car - ry me home, A
F7 B♭ C dm G7 C7 F
band of an - gels com- in' af - ter me, Com- in' for to car - ry me home.

Moderato
mf legato cantabile
4
7
poco cresc.

11
f
mf
15
decresc.
mp
3
19
22
26
3

30
12
3
sub. p
33
mp espr.
poco cresc.
38
p
42
cresc.
cresc.
47
poco rit.
Tempo I
8va
sub. p
poco rit.

H-1093 Budapest, Vámház krt. 5.
Responsible co-editor: János Gyulai Gaál

K 166

Distributed worldwide by Tandem Verlag GmbH
Im Mühlenbruch 1, D-53639 Königswinter

Printed in EU

ISBN 3-8331-1349-9

IN DIESER REIHE ERSCHEINEN:
ADDITIONAL TITLES AVAILABLE IN THIS SERIES:
DANS CETTE SERIE:

Bach, J.S.:
Das wohltemperierte Klavier I
ISBN: 3-8331-1321-9
EAN: 9783 8331 13215

Bach, J.S.:
Das wohltemperierte Klavier II
ISBN: 3-8331-1322-7
EAN: 9783 8331 13222

Bach, J.S.:
Englische Suiten
ISBN: 3-8331-1323-5
EAN: 9783 8331 13239

Bach, J.S.:
Französische Suiten
ISBN: 3-8331-1324-3
EAN: 9783 8331 13246

Bach, J.S.:
Inventionen, Sinfonien, kleine Präludien und Fughetten
ISBN: 3-8331-1325-1
EAN: 9783 8331 13253

Mozart:
Sonaten I
ISBN: 3-8331-1343-X
EAN: 9783 8331 13437

Mozart:
Sonaten II
ISBN: 3-8331-1344-8
EAN: 9783 8331 13444

Mendelssohn-Bartholdy:
Lieder ohne Worte I
ISBN: 3-8331-1340-5
EAN: 9783 8331 13406

Mendelssohn-Bartholdy:
Lieder ohne Worte II
ISBN: 3-8331-1341-3
EAN: 9783 8331 13413

Mendelssohn-Bartholdy:
Lieder ohne Worte III
ISBN: 3-8331-1342-1
EAN: 9783 8331 13420

Debussy:
Children's Corner & Individual Pieces
ISBN: 3-8331-1334-0
EAN: 9783 8331 13345

Beethoven:
Sonaten I
ISBN: 3-8331-1326-X
EAN: 9783 8331 13260

Beethoven:
Sonaten II
ISBN: 3-8331-1327-8
EAN: 9783 8331 13277

Beethoven:
Sonaten III
ISBN: 3-8331-1328-6
EAN: 9783 8331 13284

Beethoven:
Sonaten IV
ISBN: 3-8331-1329-4
EAN: 9783 8331 13291

Frédéric
Chopin
ÉTUDES
URTEXT

Chopin:
Études
ISBN: 3-8331-1330-8
EAN: 9783 8331 13307

Robert
Schumann
ALBUM FÜR DIE JUGEND
KINDERSZENEN
URTEXT

Schumann:
Album f. d. Jugend /
Kinderszenen
ISBN: 3-8331-1348-0
EAN: 9783 8331 13482

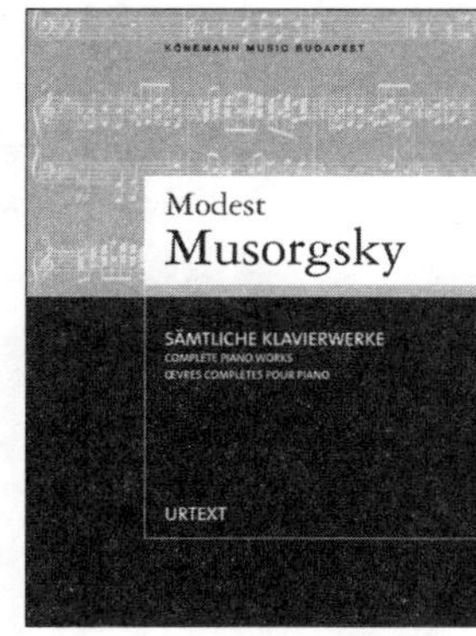
Modest
Musorgsky
SÄMTLICHE KLAVIERWERKE
URTEXT

Musorgsky:
Sämtliche Klavierwerke
ISBN: 3-8331-1345-6
EAN: 9783 8331 13451

Frédéric
Chopin
NOCTURNES
URTEXT

Chopin:
Nocturnes
ISBN: 3-8331-1331-6
EAN: 9783 8331 13314

Edvard
Grieg
LYRISCHE STÜCKE I
URTEXT

Grieg:
Lyrische Stücke I
ISBN: 3-8331-1337-5
EAN: 9783 8331 13376

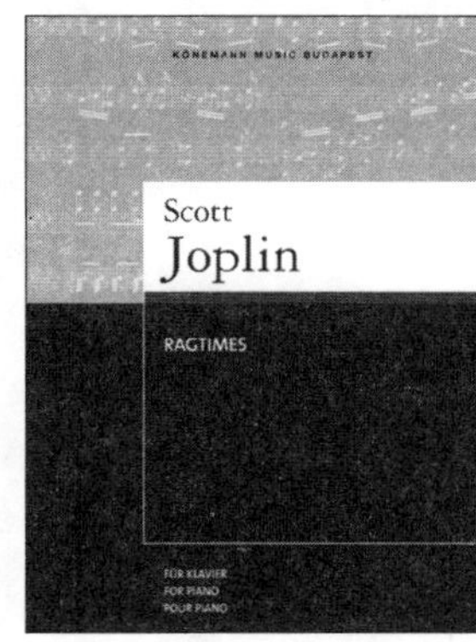
Scott
Joplin
RAGTIMES

Joplin:
Ragtimes
ISBN: 3-8331-1339-1
EAN: 9783 8331 13390

Frédéric
Chopin
VALSES
URTEXT

Chopin:
Valses
ISBN: 3-8331-1332-4
EAN: 9783 8331 13321

Edvard
Grieg
LYRISCHE STÜCKE II
URTEXT

Grieg:
Lyrische Stücke II
ISBN: 3-8331-1338-3
EAN: 9783 8331 13383

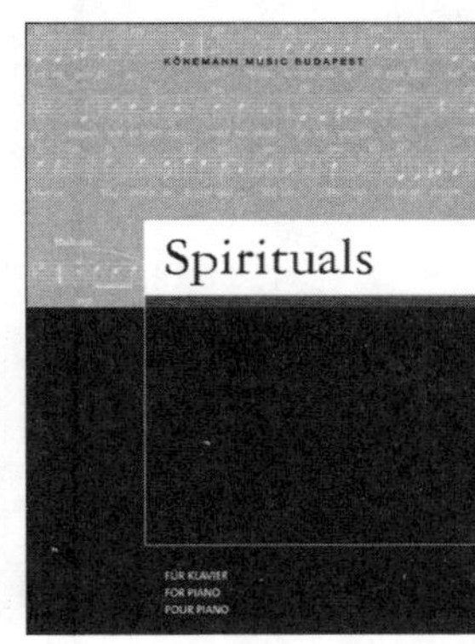
Spirituals

Spirituals
ISBN: 3-8331-1349-9
EAN: 9783 8331 13499

Franz
Schubert
KLAVIERSTÜCKE
IMPROMPTUS
MOMENTS MUSICAUX
URTEXT

Schubert:
Klavierstücke,
Impromptus,
Moments musicaux
ISBN: 3-8331-1347-2
EAN: 9783 8331 13475

Johann
Strauss
WALZER

Strauss:
Walzer
ISBN: 3-8331-1351-0
EAN: 9783 8331 13512

Alte Tänze
Early Dances
Danses anciennes
ALLEMANDE, COURANTE,
SARABANDE, GIGUE, MENUETT,
POLONAISE, WALZER ...

Alte Tänze
ISBN: 3-8331-1350-2
EAN: 9783 8331 13505

KÖNEMANN MUSIC BUDAPEST

DISTRIBUTED WORLDWIDE BY
TANDEM VERLAG GMBH · IM MÜHLENBRUCH 1 · D-53639 KÖNIGSWINTER